Beyo1 Reasonable Doubt

DISCOVERY SERIES BIBLE STUDY
For individuals or groups

Just before I graduated from seminary, I received a phone call from my eighty-year-old grandfather. He was calling to congratulate me. He asked about the kids; I asked if he had been fishing. He talked about getting the old boat fixed and in the river, and then the conversation took an unexpected turn. "Son (my grandfather calls me 'Son'), I need to ask you a question. I've been wondering for all of my life and never knew anyone to ask . . . Son, can I trust the Bible? I mean is my Bible, the one I read in English, saying the same thing the original Bible said?" When I hung up the phone that day, my grandfather wasn't a better Christian because of our conversation. Nor was he free from every doubt or question he ever had about God, Jesus, or the Bible. But he was more informed about one important issue related to his faith. This brief booklet may not answer every question or doubt you have about the Bible, but it is written with the hope that as you read you will, as my grandfather did, see that the Bible is trustworthy.

—Dennis Moles

This Discovery Series Bible Study is based on
Beyond Reasonable Doubt (Q0411), one of the popular Discovery Series booklets from
this ministry. Find out more about Discovery Series at
discoveryseries.org

Discovery House Publishers is affiliated with Our Daily Bread Ministries,
Grand Rapids, Michigan.

Requests for permission to quote from this book should be directed to:
Permissions Department, Discovery House Publishers, PO Box 3566, Grand Rapids, MI 49501,
or contact us by e-mail at permissionsdept@dhp.org

Managing Editor: Dave Branon
Study Guide questions: Dave Branon
Graphic Design: Steve Gier

COVER PHOTO:
Markus Huth via FreeImages.com

INSIDE PHOTOS:
hdm1652 via Pixabay.com, p.6; monosodium via MorgueFile.com, p.8; Alvimann via MorgueFile.com, p.14;
Ceinturion via Wikimedia Commons, p.16; Chris Ashcraft via CreationWiki.org, p.17; Georges Jansoone via
Creative Commons, p.20; Gustave Doré via Public Domain, p.22; Eric Matson via Public Domain, p.23; Public Domain, p.28;
Tamar Hayardeni via Wikemedia Commons, p.30; felixioncool via Pixabay.com, p.31; Yoav Dothan via
Wikimedia Commons, p.36; Jost Amman via Public Domain, p.38; Julia Freeman-Woolpert via FreeImages.com, p.39;
Sias van Schalkwyk via FreeImages.com, p.44; jdurham via MorgueFile.com, p.46

ISBN: 978-1-62707-335-6
Printed in the United States of America
First Printing in 2015

Table of Contents

How To Use
DISCOVERY SERIES BIBLE STUDIES

The Purpose

The Discovery Series Bible Study (DSBS) series provides assistance to pastors and lay leaders in guiding and teaching fellow Christians with lessons adapted from RBC Ministries Discovery Series booklets and supplemented with items taken from the pages of *Our Daily Bread*. The DSBS series uses the inductive study method to help Christians understand the Bible more clearly.

The Format

READ: Each DSBS book is divided into a series of lessons. For each lesson, you will read a few pages that will give you insight into one aspect of the overall study. Included in some studies will be FOCAL POINT and TIME OUT FOR THEOLOGY segments to help you think through the material. These can be used as discussion starters for group sessions.

RESPOND: At the end of the reading is a two-page STUDY GUIDE to help participants respond to and reflect on the subject. If you are the leader of a group study, ask each member to preview the STUDY GUIDE before the group gets together. Don't feel that you have to work your way through each question in the STUDY GUIDE; let the interest level of the participants dictate the flow of the discussion. The questions are designed for either group or individual study. Here are the parts of that guide:

MEMORY VERSE: A short Scripture passage that focuses your thinking on the biblical truth at hand and can be used for memorization. You might suggest memorization as a part of each meeting.

WARMING UP: A general interest question that can foster discussion (group) or contemplation (individual).

THINKING THROUGH: Questions that will help a group or a student interact with the reading. These questions help drive home the critical concepts of the book.

DIGGING IN: An inductive study of a related passage of Scripture, reminding the group or the student of the importance of Scripture as the final authority.

GOING FURTHER: A two-part wrap-up of the response: REFER suggests ways to compare the ideas of the lesson with teachings in other parts of the Bible. REFLECT challenges the group or the learner to apply the teaching in real life.

OUR DAILY BREAD: After each STUDY GUIDE session will be an *Our Daily Bread* article that relates to the topic. You can use this for further reflection or for an introduction to a time of prayer.

Go to the Leader's and User's Guide on page 47 for further suggestions about using this Discovery Series Bible Study.

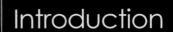

Mackenzie's Dilemma

I think I might be losing my faith," says Mackenzie.

Home for semester break, the college junior was having coffee with Terry, her former youth leader. "My doubts started at the beginning of my freshman year of college and have only gotten worse. I thought they would go away if I just prayed more or read my Bible more, but they haven't. I don't know what to do."

As a science major, Mackenzie sees too much complexity and too much fine-tuning in the universe to doubt the existence of an intelligent and purposeful creator. She still believes in God, but she struggles with the Bible. She's just not sure she can trust it to give her a clear picture of who the designer of the universe really is.

Recently, one of her literature professors spent two full weeks working through a series of lectures titled "The Bible—Mythic History or Historic Myth?"

During this section of the course, the professor attacked the reliability and authenticity of the Bible, making three specific statements that troubled her:

• **"There is no significant historical or archaeological support for believing that the Bible is historically accurate."**

• **"There is little textual evidence to support the claims of the Bible aside from a few ancient and inconsistent scraps."**

• **"Modern science has made it impossible to believe that the Bible is true and trustworthy."**

"So what do I do?" Mackenzie asks. "How do I keep believing the Bible when there are so many problems with it?"

1

Starting in the Right Place

Terry, the former youth leader, might respond to Mackenzie's concerns by reminding her that the evidences of the Bible's credibility are far greater than its problems. But what about those who are not inclined to give the Bible the benefit of the doubt? Would such people be convinced by hearing that:

> **The Bible is bluntly honest.** It records the moral and spiritual failures of those whose stories it tells. Such candor is important. Potentially

embarrassing reports written about one's own family, friends, or groups tend to be treated as an indicator of authenticity.

Jesus endorsed the Bible. He made it clear that He believed the Old Testament to be more than just national history or religious fable (Matthew 4:1–11; 5:17–19). He believed that the Scriptures were about Him—they told the story of God's love and promise of a coming Messiah (John 5:39–40).

The Bible describes itself as more than just a human book. Its timeless influence is therefore grounded not merely in the opinion of its readers, but also in the claims it makes for itself (2 Timothy 3:16; 2 Peter 1:16–21).

Those who accept that the Bible is true and trustworthy find these features of Scripture compelling. Such arguments are called *internal evidences*—using the testimony of the Bible itself to make their point. Internal evidences often reassure the faith of a believer, but just as often they fail to convince doubters that the Bible deserves to be trusted.

Suppose Mackenzie's college professor believes that newspapers are an inaccurate and untrustworthy source of information. Mackenzie disagrees with this assessment and sets out to build a case for the trustworthiness of newspapers by saying, "According to the *New York Times,* newspapers are fifty percent more likely to be accurate than Internet and television news sources. Last year the *London Times* ranked the top fifty news sources in the English-speaking world, and the *London Times* topped the list as the globe's most trustworthy news source."

> Internal evidences often reassure the faith of a believer, but just as often they fail to convince doubters that the Bible deserves to be trusted.

Would this line of reasoning be convincing? Would she be able to change her professor's mind based on the evidence? Probably not. Why? Because these arguments are based on an authority that her professor doubts.

In the same way, when those who believe the Bible set out to prove its trustworthiness using only the internal evidences, they can quickly lose credibility with those who are skeptical. This does not mean that the internal evidences are not valid. It simply means that when talking with those who doubt the reliability of Scripture, we should begin in a different place.

Evidence and the Supernatural

For many, the Bible describes a world they have never seen and cannot accept. They read about supernatural events that don't fit with the laws of nature as they understand them. This was one of the key points in Mackenzie's professor's attacks on the reliability of Scripture, and it involves an idea about knowledge and truth that needs to be explored—the often-unquestioned assumption that scientific inquiry is the most reliable basis for knowing anything about our world. Some might even say it's the *only* reliable basis.

Many would probably agree that scientific investigation has been an important means of opening up our understanding. But there is disagreement about whether it is the only or even the best way to discover truth. While some believe that the Bible is true and trustworthy even when it makes supernatural claims that cannot be scientifically tested, others are convinced

> While the skeptic is correct in his or her assertion that we cannot prove with certainty that the Bible is trustworthy, it is also true that the skeptic cannot prove that the miracles reported in the Bible are impossible.

that scientific methods are the best or only way to understand reality and determine truth. They insist that it doesn't make sense to try to embrace both scientific inquiry and the Bible as sources of truth. Their worldview makes it impossible to believe the stories of the Bible that bend or break natural laws: a virgin giving birth, a man walking on water, a person rising from the dead, or a small amount of bread and fish feeding thousands of people.

> One of the most common reasons people doubt the trustworthiness of the Bible is its miraculous claims. How can they trust a truth source, the Bible, that so obviously contradicts observable reality? Many see this as unenlightened superstition.

But while scientific inquiry gives us knowledge and measures some truth claims, can we assert that it is the *only* way we know and experience truth? Are there things we know that cannot be tested scientifically?

Can we say we know . . .

- *When we love someone?*
- *That a sunset is beautiful?*
- *That justice is better than injustice?*
- *That Abraham Lincoln was the sixteenth president of the United States?*

No doubt, questioning this last statement sounds silly, but think about it: How *do* we know that the sixteenth president of the United States was Abraham Lincoln? We know nothing about Lincoln from firsthand experience or scientific inquiry. We've never met him. We didn't vote for him.

"No," you might say, "but we have documentation—books, letters, photos, and other historical records that tell us he was the sixteenth president."

What if, despite overwhelming evidence to the contrary, I refused to accept that "Honest Abe" was president of the United States from 1861 to 1865?

In this scenario, is my doubt rational? Is it reasonable for me to hold this belief even though we cannot prove today from firsthand experience (seeing, touching, tasting, smelling, or hearing) or by an appeal to scientific inquiry that Abraham Lincoln was president? We have good reasons to believe that he was the sixteenth president of the United States. We have mountains of testimonial evidence that he was elected in 1860 and reelected in 1864, that he signed the Emancipation Proclamation, and that he was assassinated by John Wilkes Booth on April 14, 1865. This is just a sampling of the historical evidence from many reputable sources of the 1850s and 60s that makes it ludicrous to deny that Lincoln was the sixteen president.

To refuse to believe the Lincoln presidency because of a few inconsistencies in reports and possible contradictions in the reports of his whereabouts, thoughts, and political and sociological views would be irrational. Why? Because while it is *possible* that the Lincoln presidency was an elaborate hoax, it is highly *improbable*.

■ SCIENTIFIC METHOD

Simply put, the scientific method (or scientific inquiry) is this:

1. **Ask a question.**
2. **Conduct research on the question.**
3. **Propose a hypothesis based on your research.**
4. **Design an experiment to test the hypothesis.**
5. **Test the hypothesis.**
6. **Accept or reject the hypothesis based on the results of the test.**

If the hypothesis is rejected, the hypothesis should be revised and retested.

The difference between the historical record for the Lincoln presidency and the story of the Bible is clear. The record of the Lincoln presidency doesn't include claims for supernatural events as does the story of the Bible.

It's the claims of the miraculous that cause so many to discount the Bible as unreliable.

Given this, is it reasonable to claim that the Bible is trustworthy? Is there any evidence to support that claim? Is there any external evidence that supports the internal claims of the Bible?

■ FOCAL POINT

The objective is not to use human standards to prove beyond a doubt that a given book is from God, because naturally, if something is from God, it just will not conform to human standards at every turn. However, though we might not be able to track down proof for every word, by presenting a general reliability, we can point the finger at fundamental skepticism and ask whether that is the best approach.

—MATT LEFEBVRE

Starting in the Right Place

MEMORY VERSE
Matthew 5:17—

"Do not think that I
came to destroy the
Law or the Prophets.
I did not come to
destroy but to fulfill."

**To begin to see what kind of evidence is
needed to support the Bible's credibility.**

Warming Up

Do you know anyone who is skeptical about the veracity
of the Bible? If you have had conversations with that
person, what are the major objections to believing God's
Word?

Thinking Through

1. If Mackenzie were to come to you and ask, "So what do I do?" what suggestions would
you have for her?

2. On page 8, Dennis Moles suggests that the idea that "the Bible is bluntly honest" is
an evidence of the Bible's credibility. Explain how that is a compelling argument for
believability.

3. What do you think of the Abraham Lincoln analogy in regard to historical truth and
the Bible? How is that helpful in this study?

Going Further

Refer

Examine each of these passages regarding the internal evidence of the reliability of God's
Word. What confidence do they give you? What questions do they leave you with?

Matthew 4:4, 7, 10

John 5:39–40

2 Timothy 3:16

1. Peter makes a strong case for the reliability of the words of Scripture. What value in regard to his argument are these words in verse 16: "eyewitnesses of His majesty"? What is the value of eyewitnesses in any argument?

_____

_____

_____

_____

_____

2. Similarly, Peter says, "we heard this voice which came from heaven" in verse 18. What incident is Peter referring to as he speaks of being with Jesus "on the holy mountain"?

_____

_____

_____

_____

3. Continuing to make his argument for trusting the Word of God, Peter states boldly, "prophecy never came by the will of man" (v. 21). What thrilling truth can be gleaned from that statement regarding the Bible?

_____

_____

_____

16 For we did not follow cunningly devised fables when we made known to you the power and coming of our Lord Jesus Christ, but were eyewitnesses of His majesty. 17 For He received from God the Father honor and glory when such a voice came to Him from the Excellent Glory: "This is My beloved Son, in whom I am well pleased." 18 And we heard this voice which came from heaven when we were with Him on the holy mountain.

19 And so we have the prophetic word confirmed, which you do well to heed as a light that shines in a dark place, until the day dawns and the morning star rises in your hearts; 20 knowing this first, that no prophecy of Scripture is of any private interpretation, 21 for prophecy never came by the will of man, but holy men of God spoke as they were moved by the Holy Spirit.

Prayer Time ➤

Use the _Our Daily Bread_ article on the next page as a guide for a devotional and meditation time relating to the Bible.

Reflect

While internal evidence of the Bible's credibility may not sway skeptics, what power do passages such as 2 Peter 1:16–21 provide for your heart? _____

_____

Just as we have documents to show that Abraham Lincoln was once the US president, we have empirical evidence that God's Word is trustworthy. As you head into the next sessions of this study, what extra-biblical evidence do you already know about? _____

Once Upon a Time

Some people say that the Bible is just a collection of fairy tales. A boy slaying a giant. A man swallowed by a big fish. Noah's boat-building experience. Even some religious people think that these events are just nice stories with a good moral.

Jesus himself, however, spoke of Jonah and the giant fish, and Noah and the flood, as actual events: "As the days of Noah were, so also will the coming of the Son of Man be. For as in the days before the flood, they were eating and drinking, marrying and giving in marriage, until the day that Noah entered the ark, and did not know until the flood came and took them all away, so also will the coming of the Son of Man be" (Matthew 24:37–39). His return will happen when we're not expecting it.

Jesus compared Jonah's three days inside the big fish to the three days He would experience in the grave before His resurrection (Matthew 12:40). And Peter talked about Noah and the flood when he equated it to a future day when Jesus comes back (2 Peter 2:4–9).

God gave us His Word; it's a book that is filled with truth—not fairy tales. And one day we will live happily ever after with Him when Jesus comes again and receives His children to himself.

—*Cindy Hess Kasper*

▲ *This is a full-scale replica of Noah's ark, built by Johan Huibers of the Netherlands. It is o display in Dordrecht.*

JONAH 1:17—

The LORD had prepared a great fish to swallow Jonah. And Jonah was in the belly of the fish three days and three nights.

■ Read today's *Our Daily Bread* at **odb.org**

2

Historical and Archaeological Support

These hieroglyphics are part of a Hittite altar displayed in the Museum of Anatolian Civilizations, Ankara, Turkey.

hen it comes to religious literature, the uniqueness of the Bible is that the record of its events is linked to named people, times, and places. Many of these places and cultures are recognizable: Egypt, the Sinai Peninsula, Syria, Jerusalem, and Galilee. But some are ancient and obscure enough for their historicity to be doubted.

For instance, around the turn of the twentieth century, archaeologist John Garstang made a discovery that had far-reaching effects in the world of biblical studies; he discovered archaeological evidence for the Hittite Empire.

In Garstang's time, the trustworthiness of the Bible was being hotly contested. Those who questioned the Bible's inspiration and authenticity contended that the historical and archaeological evidence for the Bible's accuracy did not add up, and they cited the lack of this type of evidence for the Hittite Empire as a specific example.

Defenders of the Scriptures, for the most part, agreed with critics that the Bible's primary purpose is not to serve as a history book or scientific work, but they maintained that the Bible is historically accurate, including its reference to the existence of the Hittite Empire.

Even though other ancient literature referred to the Hittites,[1] the critics' argument convinced many until Garstang's 1908 discovery. His archaeological find exposed an ancient civilization that existed for more than four centuries (1600–1200 BC) and revealed a treasure trove of information about its people.[2] Since then, so much has been discovered about the Hittite Empire that it is now possible to study ancient Hittite culture, religion, and languages at places like the Oriental Institute of the University of Chicago.

And it's not just the Hittite evidence. Engraved stones or cylinders from other ancient civilizations verify other biblical accounts. For example, the Taylor Prism confirms the Assyrian siege of Jerusalem that the Bible describes in 2 Kings 18–19, 2 Chronicles 32, and Isaiah 36–37. The discovery of the Tel Dan Steele confirms the existence of Israel's King David. The Cyrus Cylinder records Cyrus of Persia's decree that allowed Babylonian captives to return to their homes and resume religious practices (Ezra 1). The Moabite Stone substantiates

■ Focal Point

"On the whole . . . archaeological work has unquestionably strengthened confidence in the reliability of the Scriptural record. More than one archaeologist has found his respect for the Bible increased by the experience of excavation in Palestine. Archaeology has in many cases refuted the views of modern critics."

—MILLAR BURROWS,
PROFESSOR OF ARCHAEOLOGY, YALE UNIVERSITY

the events of 2 Kings 3. The stone not only chronicles the rebellion led by Mesha, king of Moab, but it also mentions the name *Yahweh*.[3]

Historical documents also support the Bible's testimony about Jesus and the ancient church's commitment to the gospel story. Jewish and Roman historians referred to the life and works of Jesus.[4] Josephus wrote about Jesus' miracles. And Pliny the Younger, an ancient ruler, recorded that Christians in his province maintained their belief in and the worship of Jesus even when faced with death.[5]

While these examples are just a sample of the available information supporting the accuracy of the Bible, they are sufficient to contradict the skeptics' assertion that there is no significant historical or archaelogocial support for believing that the Bible is historically accurate. That claim is simply not true.

---

[1] Miram Lichtheim, *Ancient Egyptian Literature*, vol. 2. *The New Kingdom* (Berkeley: University of California Press), 57.

[2] Avraham Negev, *The Archaeological Encyclopedia of the Holy Land*, 3rd ed. (New York: Prentice Hall Press, 1990).

[3] K. A. Kitchen, *On the Reliability of the Old Testament* (Grand Rapids: Eerdmans, 2003), 34–50. See also **www.jewishencyclopedia.com/articles/10899-moabite-stone**.

[4] Josephus, *The Works of Josephus: Complete and unabridged*, trans. William Whiston (Peabody: Hendrickson, 1987).

[5] Doug Powell, *Holman QuickSource Guide to Christian Apologetics* (Nashville: Holman Reference, 2006), 164–66.

STUDY GUIDE 2
read pages 17–19

To look at how history and archaeology team up to support the believability of the Bible.

MEMORY VERSE
Matthew 24:35—

"Heaven and earth will pass away, but My words will by no means pass away."

Warming Up

What have you heard or read regarding the historical support for the Bible? What troubles you when this subject comes up?

Thinking Through

1. What was the significance of the discovery more than a century ago of historical evidence of a people group called the Hittites?

2. Discuss the importance of the Tel Dan Steele and the Cyrus Cylinder in regard to the children of Israel.

3. When you see that historians Josephus and Pliny the Younger made reference to Jesus and Christians in the first century, how does that strengthen your faith in the historicity of Christianity?

Going Further

Refer

Look at these passages for biblical information about items mentioned in this chapter:
Hittites: Joshua 1:4; Judges 1:26; 1 Kings 10:29

Dan: Joshua 19:47; Judges 18

Read the decree of Cyrus in Ezra 1:1–4. If possible, find a copy of the words of the Cyrus Cylinder online and compare the two.

1. Matthew 4:12–17 is one of numerous passages in Scripture that give actual place names that can be found in both history and the present. What is the significance for our study that verse 13 says, "Leaving Nazareth, He came and dwelt in Capernaum"?

_____

_____

_____

2. The mention of Naphtali in both passages and in others such as Joshua 19:32 and Joshua 20:7 (et al) brings it from obscurity into the light of reality. Discuss how even obscure place names have significance in historical documents.

_____

_____

_____

3. The Way of the Sea is mentioned in both passages. It is also called Via Maris—and was a major trade route. How does that fact play into this dual reference—and how does the fact that it is an actual geographic/historic entity help you in your appreciation of the Bible's credibility?

_____

_____

_____

[1] Nevertheless the gloom will not be upon her who is distressed, as when at first He lightly esteemed the land of Zebulun and the land of Naphtali, and afterward more heavily oppressed her, by the way of the sea, beyond the Jordan, in Galilee of the Gentiles.

[2] The people who walked in darkness have seen a great light; those who dwelt in the land of the shadow of death, upon them a light has shined.

[12] Now when Jesus heard that John had been put in prison, He departed to Galilee. [13] And leaving Nazareth, He came and dwelt in Capernaum, which is by the sea, in the regions of Zebulun and Naphtali, [14] that it might be fulfilled which was spoken by Isaiah the prophet, saying:

[15] "The land of Zebulun and the land of Naphtali, by the way of the sea, beyond the Jordan, Galilee of the Gentiles:

[16] The people who sat in darkness have seen a great light, and upon those who sat in the region and shadow of death light has dawned."

Prayer Time ⟩

Use the *Our Daily Bread* article on the next page as a guide for a devotional and meditation time relating to the Bible.

Reflect

When you read fiction, you may recognize place names—but you may also see names of places that the author simply makes up. Think about what you've just read about history and archaeology—and reflect on how that affects your view of a book—the Bible—that is said to be true.

_____

_____

The Bible Stands!

Unbelievers have long scoffed at the biblical story of the fall of the ancient city of Jericho. That's why I was delighted to see this headline on the front page of the newspaper: "New Study Backs Biblical Version of Jericho's Demise."

The Associated Press article began, "The walls of Jericho did come tumbling down as recounted in the Bible, according to an archaeological study." Archaeologist Bryant G. Wood of the University of Toronto said, "When we compare the archaeological evidence at Jericho with the biblical narrative describing the Israelite destruction of Jericho, we find remarkable agreement." Wood noted that the Bible places the event after spring harvest and indicates that the Israelites burned the city—both facts confirmed by the archaeological remains. Once again, archaeology bears testimony to the truthfulness of Scripture.

Our belief in the authenticity of the Bible does not depend on scientific research but on its claim to be God's Word. As 2 Timothy 3:16 tells us, "All Scripture is given by inspiration of God." We can therefore have complete confidence in what it says.

It's a fact—the walls of Jericho did indeed fall. The Bible stands!

—*Richard DeHaan*

HEBREWS 11:30—

By faith the walls of Jericho fell down after they were encircled for seven days.

■ Read today's *Our Daily Bread* at **odb.org**

3

The Preservation of the Bible

A view of the Dead Sea from a cave at Qumran in which some of the Dead Sea Scrolls were discovered.

So how do we respond to those who doubt that the Bible we read is the same as that which was originally written—or that it really is an ancient record? The truth is that the Christian Scriptures are the best-preserved documents in the history of literature. This is a bold claim. But given the evidence, it is no overstatement, and it is based on three criteria: the historical distance between the original writing and the earliest copies, the consistency of the documents, and the number of known copies.

We have evidence that the Gospels were written by apostles or in cooperation with them. Irenaeus, a disciple of Polycarp, who was a disciple of the apostle John, wrote this:

> *Matthew also issued a written Gospel among the Hebrews in their own dialect, while Peter and Paul were preaching at Rome, and laying the foundations of the Church. After their departure, Mark, the disciple and interpreter of Peter, did also hand down to us in writing what have been preached by Peter. Luke also, the companion of Paul, recorded in a book the Gospel preached by him. Afterwards, John, the disciple of the Lord, who also had leaned upon His breast, did himself publish a Gospel during his residence at Ephesus in Asia.[6]*

These claims are consistent with other early witnesses.[7] But there is even more evidence that the Old and New Testaments are accurate and that they were written when and by whom Christians claim. Today we have the Scriptures because centuries ago scribes copied the originals in order to preserve them. They paid meticulous attention to detail when they copied the text, which leads many scholars to believe that the copies can be trusted as accurate reproductions of the originals.

But what about the time that elapsed between the known copies? Critics argue that the historical distance between the time the books were first written and our oldest existing manuscripts virtually guarantees that mistakes were introduced into the text.

This argument suffered a crippling blow following the discovery of the Dead Sea Scrolls in the late 1940s to mid-1950s. The Dead Sea Scrolls are a collection of more than 950 manuscripts and text fragments. Most of these are copies of Old Testament Scriptures that date from the third century BC to the middle of the first century AD. Until this discovery, the earliest manuscripts for the Old Testament were the Masoretic Texts (MT), which dated from about AD 980. Not only did the Dead Sea Scrolls give us older copies, but they also allowed scholars to investigate the consistency between earlier and later copies. What they found was striking.

When comparing the MT copy of Isaiah 53 and copies of the same passage in the Dead Sea Scrolls, scholars found remarkable consistency. Out of the 166 Hebrew *words* in Isaiah 53, only 17 *letters* differ between the documents! None of these differences have any effect on the meaning of the text. Even though these documents were separated by approximately 1,000 years, their remarkable similarity demonstrates that great care was indeed taken to copy and preserve the biblical text.[8]

The Dead Sea Scrolls are strong evidence for the accuracy of the biblical text. But this isn't the only evidence. Comparing the number of biblical manu-

● Focal Point

In any publication, small variations creep in, but the variations are so small that we can take for granted that any reputable book quoting an ancient document is doing so accurately. Actually, the Bible is the most accurate ancient writing in existence.

—JOHN F. WALVOORD
WHAT WE BELIEVE

scripts in existence today with the number of existing manuscripts of other ancient texts also supports the integrity of the Scriptures.

Homer wrote the *Iliad* in approximately 800 BC, and there are 643 known Greek copies, or portions of copies, still in existence. The earliest of these is a partial copy that dates to approximately 400 BC. The first complete text dates to the thirteenth century. This means that the time between the actual writing of the *Iliad* and the oldest partial copy in existence is about 400 years, and the time between the actual writing and the first full copy is 2,100 years.

Four hundred years may sound like a lot of time. But in the preservation of ancient literature, 400 years is brief. And 643 copies is substantial when compared with the number of copies of other ancient works. There are eight copies of Herodotus' *History*, and the time between the original and the earliest copy is 1,350 years. There are ten copies of Caesar's *Gallic Wars*, and the gap is 1,000 years. There are twenty copies of Tacitus' *Annals*, seven copies of

Pliny Secundus' Natural History, and twenty copies of Livy's *History of Rome*, with historical distances of 1,000, 750, and 400 years respectively.[9] Yet despite the length of time between the original writings and the earliest copies, virtually no one questions the validity, accuracy, or authenticity of these documents.

In light of this information, it is reasonable to assert that if the biblical documents exceed these numbers, we have more than sufficient evidence that the Bible we read today is the same as when it was written.

So how does the Scripture fare in comparison to these other ancient works? Currently, we have approximately 5,500 full or partial copies of the New Testament. One complete copy of the New Testament can be dated to within 225 years of the original writing. The earliest confirmed New Testament Scriptures date back to AD 114. This means that the historical distance between our earliest copies and the date of the original writing is, at

■ Focal Point

The Old Testament books were written primarily in Hebrew. They were recorded either on papyrus or parchment. When a copy wore out, a new copy was made. The old one was destroyed.

But that was not an easy task. . . . It had to be done by hand. Stringent rules were followed by the scribes to keep errors from creeping in. The methods used by the scribes had been followed for centuries, from AD 500–900. These dedicated Hebrew scholars had an elaborate counting system for assuring accuracy. First, they would count all the letters on a page. Then, when they finished copying the page, they would count the letters on the copy to see if the numbers agreed. . . . If the counts did not agree, they would destroy the copy they had just worked over so laboriously and start again.

most, 50 years. It is "at most" because Dr. Daniel Wallace and a team of researchers from the Center for the Study of New Testament Manuscripts believe they have located a text fragment from the gospel of Mark that dates back to the first century.

When compared with other ancient works, the textual evidence for the Christian Scriptures is remarkable. Research demonstrates that the Bible stands alone as the most thoroughly authenticated document in the history of ancient literature.

---

[6] A. Roberts, J. Donaldson, & A. C. Coxe (eds.), *The Ante-Nicene Fathers*, vol.1, *The Apostolic Fathers with Justin Martyr and Irenaeus* (Buffalo, NY: Christian Literature Company), 414.

[7] Josh McDowell, *The New Evidence that Demands a Verdict* (Nashville: Thomas Nelson, 1999), 53–55).

[8] Norman L. Geisler and William E. Nix, *A General Introduction to the Bible* (Chicago: Moody Press, 1986), 196, 261-70, 351-85.

[9] Craig L. Blomberg, *Jesus and the Gospels: An Introduction and Survey* (Nashville: B&H Academic, 2009). 424-44. See also McDowell, New Evidence, 38.

[10] Dan Wallace, "Earliest Manuscript of the New Testament Discovered?" The Center for the Study of New Testament Manuscripts, last accessed December 26, 2012, **www.csntm.org/NewsArchive/2012/2/10/ EarliestManuscriptsoftheNewTestamentDiscovered**.

STUDY GUIDE

read pages 23–27

To get a glimpse of the miraculous ways God's Word has been preserved through the millennia.

MEMORY VERSE

1 Thessalonians 2:13— "We also thank God continually because, when you received the word of God, . . . you accepted it not as the word of men, but as it actually is, the word of God" (NIV).

Warming Up

Do you enjoy old books? Perhaps you have a book in your personal library that dates back 100 years or so. While that seems exciting, talk about the miracle of having a book that is more than 2,000 years old on your shelf—the Bible.

Thinking Through

1. Dennis Moles says, "The Christian Scriptures are the best-preserved documents in the history of literature" (page 23). Why does this matter? What is the value of proving the careful preservation of this book over long periods of time?

2. What has been the value of the discovery of the Dead Sea Scrolls in Israel in the mid-twentieth century as it relates to the Bible?

3. What, in layman's terms, is the value for Bible believers of the arguments relating to manuscripts, the number of copies, and the dates of the earliest copies?

Going Further

Refer

What comfort do you find in these verses as they relate to God's preservation of His Word for us?

Isaiah 40:8

Mark 1:2; Mark 9:12; Mark 11:17

Romans 15:4

1. Even in Paul's day, there were attempts at forgery of his letters (see 2 Thessalonians 2:2). What did Paul do in Galatians 6 and Colossians 4 to verify that his words were authentic?

2. Notice Jesus' repeated use of the statement, "It is written" (Matthew 4:4–11). What does His use of those words tell us about the permanency of God's written Word?

3. What confidence do Jesus' words in Mark 13 give you regarding the preservation of Scripture?

Galatians 6:11

See with what large letters I have written to you with my own hand!

Colossians 4:18

This salutation by my own hand—Paul. Remember my chains. Grace be with you. Amen.

Matthew 4:4–6

⁴ But He answered and said, "It is written, 'Man shall not live by bread alone, but by every word that proceeds from the mouth of God.'"

⁵ Then the devil took Him up into the holy city, set Him on the pinnacle of the temple, ⁶ and said to Him, "If You are the Son of God, throw Yourself down. For it is written:

'He shall give His angels charge over you,' and, 'In their hands they shall bear you up, Lest you dash your foot against a stone.'"

Mark 13:31

Heaven and earth will pass away, but My words will never pass away.
—JESUS

Prayer Time ▶

Use the *Our Daily Bread* article on the next page as a guide for a devotional and meditation time relating to the Bible.

Reflect

As you look back at the facts presented about textual preservation, which of these evidences do you think you could use in talking to a friend about the Bible's reliability?

▲ A portion of the *Silver Scrolls text from Numbers 6:* "Yahweh make his face shine upon you, and be gracious to you."

The Silver Scrolls

The Bible has been wonderfully and accurately preserved. Copies of portions of the New Testament dating to within 50 years of the original manuscripts have been found, and they coincide with what we have today.

An archaeological report in the magazine *Discovery* contained amazing findings about the Old Testament. Before the discovery of the Dead Sea Scrolls in 1947, the oldest Hebrew manuscripts dated about AD 980. The Dead Sea Scrolls, in startling agreement with the Masoretic text, dated to about 150 BC. But now archaeologists have discovered a pair of tiny silver scrolls that date back to about 600 BC! While digging at the site of a fifth-century church in Jerusalem, researchers found an old Roman cemetery. Exploring still deeper, they found a burial cave containing the scrolls. Very carefully, less than a hundredth of an inch at a time, the scrolls were unrolled. On each of them appeared an excerpt from the book of Numbers that included the word *Jehovah*. And these scrolls date back to the days before the Babylonian exile, earlier than liberal scholars supposed that the Pentateuch had even been written!

Discoveries like that strengthen the faith Christians already have. But when a secular magazine like *Discovery* reports such a find, it speaks to a skeptical and disbelieving world as well. The silver scrolls reaffirm our confidence that the Bible can be trusted as the inspired Word of God.

—*David Egner*

ISAIAH 40:8—

The grass withers, the flower fades, but the word of our God stands forever.

■ Read today's *Our Daily Bread* at **odb.org**

4

Modern Science Has Not Disproven the Bible

As mentioned earlier, many people find it impossible to accept the Bible as true because they cannot reconcile the miracles recorded in the Bible with the conclusions of modern science. This reflects a naturalistic worldview, which assumes that things are not real, knowable, or trustworthy unless they can be tested and measured scientifically or experienced firsthand. This view is also called *scientism*.

This line of reasoning has led many naturalistic thinkers to arrive at the belief that science has disproven the Bible. They assume that because some of the Bible's claims are scientifically immeasurable, the Bible cannot be true.

Several years ago I pastored a small church in central Ohio. During that time my wife and I met Chris and Kathy, who both taught in the biology department of a local college. Our two sons and their two sons attended the same elementary school, and as our boys became fast friends, so did we. Chris and I would often meet for coffee to discuss questions relating to science and religion. But it was Kathy who posed a question that may prove helpful in this discussion about the compatibility of science and miracles.

> Many people find it impossible to accept the Bible as true because they cannot reconcile the miracles recorded in the Bible with the conclusions of modern science.

The birthday party for our younger son, Caleb, was in full swing. Close to a dozen kindergartners were there to help him celebrate. In the middle of this barely controlled chaos, Kathy, whose son was among the sugar-fueled horde, turned to Amy and me and said, "I have a question, but I don't want to offend you." After we assured her that we were hard to offend, she said, "You're both intelligent people, and Amy, you're a nurse. How is it that you believe in the virgin birth?"

For Kathy this was a real and well-intentioned question. How could two educated people—one with a college degree in science—believe that a virgin could have a baby? She was not trying to trap us or drag us into a debate; she was genuinely trying to understand how we could believe something so obviously impossible.

At that moment, Amy and I did two things that seemed to surprise Kathy. First, we affirmed her skepticism. We told her that we too believe that it is *scientifically* impossible for a virgin to have a baby. And second, we tried to address the real issue that lurked behind her question: How can you trust the Bible (or a religious system) when science (in this case, the reproductive system) contradicts it?

Our answer to this question is not found in the Bible itself but in the God the Bible reveals. We believe in the virgin birth not just because the Bible said it happened, but because we believe that the God of the Bible is able to make it happen—that He is not bound by natural law. This may seem intellectually lazy, but it is the crux of the issue. We believe something impossible happened—in this case, the virgin

> If there is no God, there can be no construct for miracles, and if there are no miracles, something is incapable of springing from nothing. And if something cannot spring from nothing, then the naturalist has no way of explaining how we all got here in the first place.

■ Focal Point

Every means of *acquiring knowledge* has its limits. The scientific method advances knowledge by collecting data via experimentation and observation. This system of acquisition is helpful in answering the question of how something functions but often falls short when answering the question of why it does what it does instead of doing something else.

birth—because we believe that God, himself the creator of the laws of nature, has the prerogative and power to work outside of them.

Interestingly, those who hold a naturalistic view of the world hold some unscientific truth claims of their own. For example, when it comes to the origin of the universe, they believe that something—everything actually—came from nothing. They say that time and chance caused life to emerge from nothingness. Some atheists feel so strongly about the truth of "something from nothing" that they repeatedly insist that the universe is a completely random place. They claim that there cannot be a design because of their deeply held belief that there is no designer. If there is a design, there must be a designer. No matter how fine-tuned the universe appears, it is still a random place because there is no designer.[11]

> It is possible that God has established "laws" we know nothing about to govern and make "miracles" happen.

Why does this matter? Because at some level we all believe and claim to know things that cannot be proven scientifically. Everyone has faith in something. Those who believe the Bible do not disbelieve the laws of nature; they simply believe that miracles—exceptions to those laws—are possible.

The truth is that everyone—those who trust the Bible and those who don't—believes many things that cannot be tested or proven. Science is simply not capable of answering every question. It cannot explain morality or provide a basis for making moral judgments. It cannot tell us what is beautiful nor can it tell us why justice is preferred over injustice. Science does not prove mathematical truths—it assumes them to function. And most intriguingly, science cannot validate the scientific method. Even the statement "science has disproven the Bible" is a claim that cannot be proven scientifically. To believe that it has is to believe something that is not scientifically verifiable.

Has modern science made it impossible to believe the Bible? No. Science simply tells us that there are no natural explanations for the miraculous claims of the Bible. But when we think about it, there are no natural or scientific explanations for love either, yet no one would say that science has disproven love. It's just not something science can do.

---

[11] Alvin Plantinga, "The Dawkins Confusion: Naturalism 'Ad Absurdum': A Review of Richard Dawkins' *The God Delusion*," in *God Is Great, God Is Good: Why Belief in God Is Reasonable and Responsible*, ed. William Lane Craig and Chad Meister (Downers Grove: IVP, 2009), 247-58.

4 Science Hasn't Disproven the Bible

STUDY GUIDE
read pages 31–35

MEMORY VERSE
Acts 2:22—

"Jesus of Nazareth, a Man attested by God to you by miracles, wonders, and signs which God did through Him in your midst, as you yourselves also know."

To reason properly with those who say that the Bible and modern science disagree.

Warming Up

Have you watched skeptics such as Bill Nye discuss their view of the Bible? If you have seen these people espouse their views, how have you reacted to their arguments against accepting the reliability of the Bible?

Thinking Through

1. If you have experienced teachers or professors who "assume that because some of the Bible's claims are scientifically immeasurable the Bible cannot be true" (page 32), who did you turn to for help in refuting their arguments? What have you heard that can help others facing such a situation?

2. Discuss Dennis Moles' statement: "Our answer to this question is not found in the Bible itself but in the God the Bible reveals" (page 33). How is that line of reasoning helpful? What kinds of questions does it not answer?

3. The "something from nothing" argument Dennis Moles presents on page 34 is at the center of both the biblicist's and the atheist's argument. The crux of the matter entails figuring out how something came from nothing. What gives credence to the biblical view on this?

Going Further

Refer

Discuss the implications of the following verses as they relate to the idea of God and His ability to do the miraculous.

Job 38:4–7

Job 40:2

Job 42:2

1. For those who believe that God created the earth and all that we see, Psalm 19:1 not only makes sense but it also provides an affirmation of God's greatness. From what you have seen from the scientific findings in astronomy, in what ways do the heavens declare God's glory?

2. If the earth is indeed God's creation, then what great message is verse 4 referring to when it says "their line has gone out through all the earth . . . to the end of the world"? (See Romans 10:17–18.)

3. In a majestic metaphor, verses 4 through 6 portray both the course of the sun across the sky and what other picture?

¹ The heavens declare the glory of God; and the firmament shows His handiwork.

² Day unto day utters speech, and night unto night reveals knowledge.

³ There is no speech nor language where their voice is not heard.

⁴ Their line has gone out through all the earth, and their words to the end of the world.

In them He has set a tabernacle for the sun, ⁵ which is like a bridegroom coming out of his chamber, and rejoices like a strong man to run its race.

⁶ Its rising is from one end of heaven, and its circuit to the other end; and there is nothing hidden from its heat.

Prayer Time ▶

Use the *Our Daily Bread* article on the next page as a guide for a devotional and meditation time relating to the Bible.

Reflect

How does this argument set with you? Does it make sense to you to consider that neither the scientist nor the biblicist can prove the unexplainable?

The Press and the Bible

▲ *This 1568 illustration shows a Gutenberg-style press in operation. A du[] of pressmen like this could generate about 3,600 pages a day.*

Secrecy, lawsuits, and the latest technological advances are part of a news item some have called "the greatest achievement of the past 1,000 years." This isn't a recent story of spy satellites or computer programs. It's the story behind Johannes Gutenberg's first-ever printing press—in 1455!

Gutenberg had tried to keep his invention top secret until it was completed, but a lawsuit by heirs of one of his investors revealed what he was working on. His press was a technological marvel that would make possible the mass printing of literature.

When Gutenberg finished his press, the first book he printed was the Bible. That single event would eventually make the Bible by far the most widely distributed book in the world! Prior to 1455, it had been preserved by making meticulous one-at-a-time copies, but since then the Bible has been mass-produced.

Why has this one book attracted so much attention? Why was it Gutenberg's first choice? And why are millions still printed every year? It's simple—the Bible is a supernatural book, the written revelation of God to man. God has inspired and preserved it, and He continues to lead people to develop new ways to spread its remarkable message of salvation.

Thank You, Lord, for the press and the Bible!

—*Dave Branon*

ISAIAH 40:8—

The word of our God stands forever.

■ Read today's
Our Daily Bread at
odb.org

38

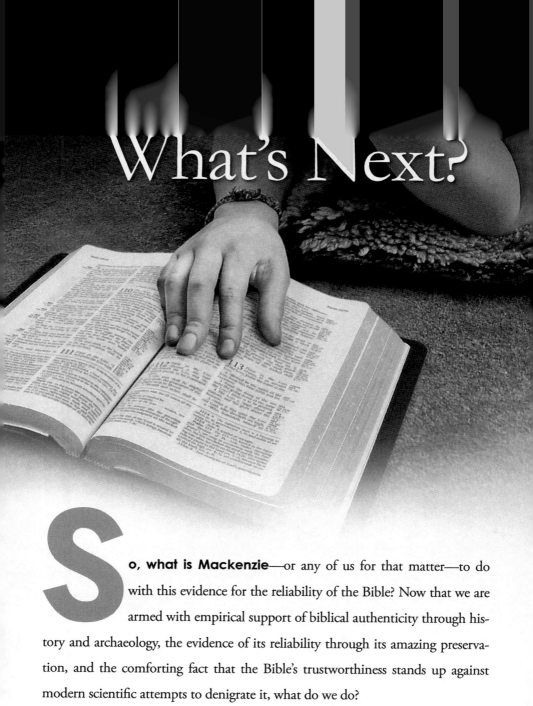

What's Next?

So, what is Mackenzie—or any of us for that matter—to do with this evidence for the reliability of the Bible? Now that we are armed with empirical support of biblical authenticity through history and archaeology, the evidence of its reliability through its amazing preservation, and the comforting fact that the Bible's trustworthiness stands up against modern scientific attempts to denigrate it, what do we do?

Examine and Live By Its Truths

Many parents have watched in pain as they have seen one of their children turn from the truths, promises, and hope offered in God's Word. Although Mom and Dad tried to instill the valuable lessons of scriptural teaching into the life of their child, that son or daughter decided to reject those truths and live a life outside of God's helpful teachings and promises. Thinking he or she knows better, this person may have chosen, for example, drunkenness over sobriety (Ephesians 5:18); sexual immorality over purity (1 Corinthians 6:18), slothfulness over industry (Proverbs 18:9), or any number of other negative

● Focal Point

The Bible has proven itself to be trustworthy in its impact on society and on individuals. Its power to change lives is seen wherever it has been taken by messengers of the gospel.

CAN I REALLY TRUST THE BIBLE?

lifestyle choices the Bible counsels us to avoid. Or worse yet, this person decided to reject the offer of eternal salvation that is the central point of the biblical story.

As many parents who have been in those situations can testify, it didn't work out very well for those children. As they moved into their adult years and as they turned their back on God's truth and teachings in this Book we can trust, they faced insurmountable obstacles of their own making. This is heartbreaking for the parents. Sometimes the adult child cannot find a way to extricate himself or herself from these problems. This alienation from biblical teachings, which often results in pain and confusion, reminds us of the value of living according to the wisdom of the Bible.

But there is always hope for every person on this earth—because of the ultimate truth found in the pages of Scripture: The truth about the greatest supernatural miracle of all time: the birth, life, death, and resurrection of Jesus Christ. This is the ultimate story of the Bible and its ultimate message: Forgiveness and an abundant life are available to all.

If we need to have a reason to believe that the Bible has been preserved for us down through the millennia, it is that God superintended its preservation so we today and those yet to come can know the eternal and unending love He has for us as shown by Jesus' sacrificial death for us on the cross.

Also, the author of this book that has been so well preserved for us has put in these pages instructions for how to live an abundant life of dedication to Him.

Our creator is the One best equipped to tell us how to make life work! And He used the Bible as a means of telling us about how to have life and to live it more abundantly (John 10:10). We would be foolish to reject what this Book tells us.

While we may not be able to convince every skeptic of the Bible's authenticity, those of us who live by it, who have accepted its message, and who know the author personally understand the inescapable value of its pages. We want so much for others to enjoy the life—both now and to come—promised in its pages.

What's next for us is to bask in the glow of its incomparable message and

● Focal Point

In a very real sense, the Bible is a book about every one of us. As we get to know its characters, we will keep coming face to face with ourselves. As we observe its people in their experiences, we will see our own experiences mirrored before us. And as we come to grips with its insights and wisdom, we will see that it is the very wisdom we need to live successfully in our contemporary world.

—DAVE EGNER
KNOWING GOD THROUGH THE WHOLE BIBLE

honor its author by living for Him. And as we do, people will see the truth of God's Word lived out in our lives—and perhaps sample it for themselves.

Trust Its Ultimate Message

The Most Compelling Reason to Trust the Bible

I know I love my wife. I know a beautiful sunset when I see one. Though I have never been there, I know that the Great Wall of China exists. And I know that the Bible is true and trustworthy.

If you have come to this book looking for certainty and ironclad arguments, we don't have them. I cannot prove beyond all doubt that the Bible is worthy of your trust and belief any more that I can prove to you that love is real or that justice is better than injustice. But after weighing the evidence, I can confidently claim that I know the Bible is true. The cumulative case for the trustworthiness of the Bible is just too convincing to reject it.

- **Is the Bible honest?** Yes. Historical and archaeological discoveries corroborate its story.

- **Does the Bible itself claim to be more than just a human book?** Yes. God has not only inspired its composition but also through the centuries has ensured its preservation.

- **Did Jesus really endorse the Scriptures?** Yes, He did. Not only did He endorse them, but He also embodied them. And this is the most compelling reason to trust the Bible.

In the pages of the Bible we encounter the most extravagant love story ever told. The God of the universe—the creator and designer of everything—chose to become a human in order to restore the relationship we willfully broke when we chose to sin.

God created a good world, but when humans sinned and kept on sinning we brought separation and distance between the Creator and His creation. But

God was unwilling to allow that separation to continue indefinitely, so He did something for us that we could not do for ourselves. He closed the gap of sin and separation through the life, death, and resurrection of Jesus Christ. We could not ascend to where He is so He descended in the person of Jesus Christ to where we are.

Are there good historical, textual, and philosophical reasons to believe that the Bible is trustworthy? Absolutely. But the most compelling reason to trust the Bible is its message of reconciliation and grace. It's not just good news—it's the best possible news.

5 What's Next?

STUDY GUIDE
read pages 39–43

To begin to sense the practical value of trusting the Bible.

MEMORY VERSE
Hebrews 4:12—

"For the word of God is living and powerful . . . piercing even to the division of soul and spirit."

Warming Up

Have you experienced the heartbreak of seeing someone reject the God who is revealed in the Holy Scriptures— and then fumble through life not realizing the self-inflicted pain their rejection is causing? How has that evidenced itself?

Thinking Through

1. Perhaps the items mentioned in the first paragraph of page 40 are not the ones you've seen people struggle with as they reject Scripture. What are some others that indicate a lack of belief that God's Word is true and reliable?

2. What have you found to be the best ways to help others accept God's truth as worthy of our trust—especially in lifestyle issues?

3. Dennis Moles says, "In the pages of the Bible we encounter the most extravagant love story ever told" (page 42). Since that is true, why do so many people view God differently —not as a God of love and compassion?

Going Further

Refer

What do these verses help you see about the credibility of God's Word?

Matthew 12:38–42

2 Timothy 3:16–17

Romans 15:4

Psalm 119:10–11

1. We see the essence of love in Philippians 2:5–8—the realization of God's great love story as recorded in the Bible. What is Paul asking the reader to do in verses 5 and 6?

> ⁵ Let this mind be in you which was also in Christ Jesus, ⁶ who, being in the form of God, did not consider it robbery to be equal with God, ⁷ but made Himself of no reputation, taking the form of a bondservant, and coming in the likeness of men. ⁸ And being found in appearance as a man, He humbled Himself and became obedient to the point of death, even the death of the cross.

2. In verse 7, Paul tells us of Jesus' willingness to take on the "likeness of men." This booklet touches on the idea of miracles. What is most amazing about the miracle of the incarnation?

3. The great love story of the Bible leads to a death. Can you explain how this "death on a cross" (v. 8) is the event that represents the central theme of all 66 books of the Bible? How does this idea of a central theme speak to the Bible's credibility?

Prayer Time ➤

Use the *Our Daily Bread* article on the next page as a guide for a devotional and meditation time relating to the Bible.

Reflect

Like no other book ever written, the Bible provides not only wisdom by which to live this life but also a plan for eternal salvation. Think about how special this makes the Bible—especially when compared with other "holy" books.

When do you feel most touched in your spirit by the Bible? What about it leads you to know in your heart that it is true?

One Amazing Letter

Once in a while my wife and I open the mail to find a letter with no words on it. When we take the "letter" out of the envelope, we see a piece of paper with nothing more on it than a colorful mark made with a felt pen. Those "letters" warm our hearts because they're from our preschool granddaughter Katie, who lives in another state. Even without words, these letters tell us that she loves us and is thinking about us.

We all cherish letters from those we love and those who love us. That's why there is so much encouragement in the fact that our heavenly Father has given us a letter called the Bible. The value of Scripture goes beyond its words of power, challenge, and wisdom. Amid all of the stories, teaching, and guidance this Book provides, the overriding idea is that God loves us and has planned our rescue. It tells us of His love in overseeing our existence (Psalm 139), meeting our needs (Matthew 6:31–34), comforting us (2 Corinthians 1:3–4), and saving us through the sacrifice of His Son, Jesus (Romans 1:16–17).

You are loved beyond imagination. God says so in His inspired and inspiring message to you. No wonder the psalmist wrote, "I will not forget Your word" (Psalm 119:16). It is one amazing letter!

—*Dave Branon*

Psalm 119:16—
I will delight myself in Your statutes; I will not forget Your word.

■ Read today's
Our Daily Bread at
odb.org

46

● LEADER'S and USER'S GUIDE

Overview of Lessons: Beyond Reasonable Doubt

Pulpit Sermon Series (for pastors and church leaders)

Although the Discovery Series Bible Study is primarily for personal and group study, pastors may want to use this material as the foundation for a series of messages on this important issue. The suggested topics and their corresponding texts from the Overview of Lessons above can be used as an outline for a sermon series.

DSBS User's Guide (for individuals and small groups)

Individuals—Personal Study
• Read the designated pages of the book.
• Carefully consider the study questions, and write out answers for each.

Small Groups—Bible-Study Discussion
• To maximize the value of the time spent together, each member should do the lesson work prior to the group meeting.
• Recommended discussion time: 45 minutes.
• Engage the group in a discussion of the questions—seeking full participation from each member.

Note To The Reader

The publisher invites you to share your response to the message of this book by writing Discovery House, P.O. Box 3566, Grand Rapids, MI 49501, USA.
For information about other Discovery House books, music, videos, or DVDs, contact us at the same address or call 1–800–653–8333. Find us on the Internet at **dhp.org** or send e-mail to **books@dhp.org**.